SCAT! SCAT!

Val Marshall • Bronwyn Tester
illustrated by Susie Donlen

THE WRIGHT ENRICHMENT READING

Mrs. Mountain!
Mrs. Mountain!
There are ants in the room!

Sweep them out!
Sweep them out!
They'll tickle our toes.

Mrs. Mountain!
Mrs. Mountain!
There's a fly in the room!

Catch it!
Catch it!
It'll bring in all its friends.

Mrs. Mountain!
Mrs. Mountain!
There's a bee in the room!

Look out!
Look out!
Don't let it sting you!

Mrs. Mountain!
Mrs. Mountain!
There's a mouse in the room!

Chase it!
Chase it!
Right out the door!

Mrs. Mountain!
Mrs. Mountain!
There's a cat in the room!

Scat!
Scat!
You naughty cat!

Mrs. Mountain!
Mrs. Mountain!
There's a dog in the room!

Get out!
Get out!
You don't belong here.

Mrs. Mountain!
Mrs. Mountain!
There's an elephant in the room!

Sit him down.
Sit him down.

Read him a story!